Collins Primary Maths
Pupil Book 1

Series Editor: Peter Clarke

Authors: Andrew Edmondson, Elizabeth Jurgensen,
Jeanette Mumford, Sandra Roberts

Contents

Topic	Objective	Pages
Place value, ordering and rounding (whole numbers)	To read and write whole numbers to at least 10 000 in figures and words, and know what each digit represents To round any positive integer less than 1000 to the nearest 10 or 100	5, 6
Measures: (length)	To record estimates and readings from scales to a suitable degree of accuracy To suggest suitable units and measuring equipment to estimate or measure length: record metres and centimetres using decimals and other measurements using mixed units To convert up to 1000 centimetres to metres, and vice versa To know the equivalent of one half, one quarter, three quarters and one tenth of 1 kilometre in m, 1 metre in cm or mm	7, 18, 19, 20, 21
Understanding addition and subtraction/Mental calculation strategies (+ and −)	To consolidate understanding of the relationship between + and −	8, 51
Mental calculation strategies (+)/Pencil and paper procedures (+)	To identify near doubles, using known doubles To use informal pencil and paper methods to support, record or explain additions: empty number line	9, 10
Pencil and paper procedures (+)/Rapid recall of addition and subtraction facts	To use informal pencil and paper methods to support, record or explain additions/subtractions: adding the most significant digits first; compensation (add too much, take off); adding the least significant digits, preparing for "carrying"	11, 12, 13, 52, 53
Pencil and paper procedures (−)/Checking results of calculations	To use informal pencil and paper methods to support, record or explain subtractions: compensation (take too much, add back)	14
Problems involving money	To use all four operations to solve word problems involving numbers in money using one or more steps, including converting pounds to pence and vice versa	15
Problems involving "real life" and money/Making decisions	To use addition and subtraction to solve word problems involving numbers in money/numbers in "real life" using one or more steps To use × and ÷ to solve word problems involving numbers in "real life" and money, using one or more steps	16, 17, 40, 45
Measures: (length)/Problems involving length/Making decisions	To use all four operations to solve word problems involving numbers in measures (length), using one or more steps, including converting metres and centimetres and vice versa	22
Measures: (perimeter)	To measure and calculate the perimeter and area of rectangles and other simple shapes, using counting methods and standard units (cm)	23
Shape and space: (2D)/Reasoning about shapes	To recognise equilateral and isosceles triangles To describe and visualise 3D shapes, including the tetrahedron	24, 25, 26

	To classify polygons using criteria such as number of right angles, whether or not they are regular, symmetry properties	
Shape and space: (position and direction)	To recognise positions and directions: for example, describe and find the position of a point on a grid of squares where the lines are numbered	27
Measures: (area and perimeter)/Reasoning about shapes	To measure and calculate the area of rectangles and other simple shapes, using counting methods	28, 29, 30
Properties of numbers and number sequences	To recognise and extend number sequences formed by counting from any number in steps of constant size: (2s, 4s); count on in steps of 25 to 500 To recognise odd and even numbers up to 1000, and some of their properties, including the outcome of sums or differences of pairs of odd/even numbers	31, 32, 33
Reasoning about numbers	To solve mathematical problems or puzzles, recognise simple patterns and relationships, generalise and predict. Suggest extensions by asking "What if…?"	34, 35
Understanding multiplication and division/Rapid recall…/Mental calculation …/Checking results	To know by heart multiplication facts for the 2, 3, 4 5 and 10 times tables To extend understanding of the operations of $\times$ and $\div$ and their relationship to each other and to + and – To derive quickly doubles of all whole numbers to 50 To multiply and divide whole numbers by 10 To use doubling and halving, starting from known facts: to multiply by 20, multiply by 10 then double, 42 To find the 8 times table facts by doubling the 4 times table To halve two–digit numbers by halving the tens first; find quarters by halving them	36, 37, 41, 42, 43, 44
Pencil and paper procedures ($\div$)	Approximate first: use informal pencil and paper methods to support, record or explain	39
Fractions and decimals	To recognise simple fractions that are several parts of a whole, such as $\frac{2}{3}$ or $\frac{5}{8}$ and mixed numbers such as $5\frac{3}{4}$ To begin to relate fractions to division and find simple fractions such as $\frac{1}{2}$, $\frac{1}{4}$, $\frac{1}{3}$, $\frac{1}{5}$, $\frac{1}{10}$ of numbers or quantities To recognise simple fractions that are several parts of a whole, such as $\frac{2}{3}$ or $\frac{5}{8}$	46, 47, 48, 49, 50
Measures: (time)/Problems involving measures (time)	To read the time from an analogue clock to the nearest minute and from a12–hour digital clock To use, read and write the vocabulary related to time To choose and use appropriate number operations and appropriate ways of calculating	54, 55
Organising and interpreting data	To solve a problem by collecting quickly, organising, representing and interpreting data in table, charts, graphs and diagrams, including those generated by a computer, for example: tally charts and frequency tables	56, 57, 58, 59, 60, 61, 62, 63, 64

Acknowledgements

The publisher would like to thank the following for their valuable comments and advice when trialling and reviewing Collins Primary Maths $\boxed{4}$ materials.

Concetta Cino – Barrow Hill Junior School, London
Mrs B Crank – Heron Hill County Primary, Kendal, Cumbria
Elizabeth Fairhead – Puttenham C of E School, Guildford, Surrey
Mrs D Kelley – Green Lane First School, Bradford
Alison Lowe – Goddard Park Primary School, Swindon
Sarah Nower – Watchetts Junior School, Camberley, Surrey
Miss M Richards – Birchfield Primary School, Birmingham
Mrs S Simco – Heron Hill County Primary, Kendal, Cumbria
Janice Turk – Sacred Heart Junior School, London
Chris Wilson – Woodville School, Leatherhead, Surrey

Footprint figures

Refresher

1 Make the number from its parts. 2000 + 500 + 40 + 6 makes 2546

a 6000 + 900 + 20 + 4 makes ▭

b 3000 + 200 + 90 + 7 makes ▭

c 4000 + 200 makes ▭

2 Write the number that each red digit represents. 5874 ___800___

a 4923 _____ b 3260 _____

c 1684 _____ d 6759 _____

e 1059 _____ f 5411 _____

Practice

1 Add these parts to make a number.

a 70 8
    200 4000

b 20 5000
    3

2 Copy and complete the calculations.

a 3597 − 10 = ▭   b 8132 + 1000 = ▭

c 3000 − 100 = ▭   d 5093 − 1000 = ▭

e 6192 + 10 = ▭   f 4678 + 100 = ▭

3 Write these numbers using words.

a 2198   b 9509   c 7013   d 2003   e 6520

5

Rounding money

Refresher

1 Round the red numbers to the nearest 10.

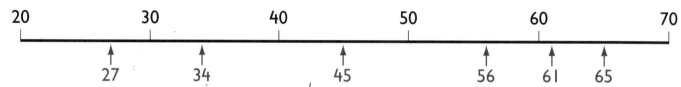

2 Round the red numbers to the nearest 10.

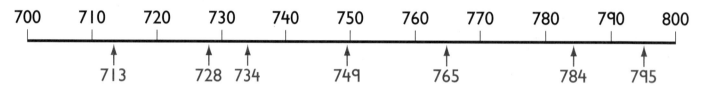

3 Now round the red numbers to the nearest 100.

Practice

Example

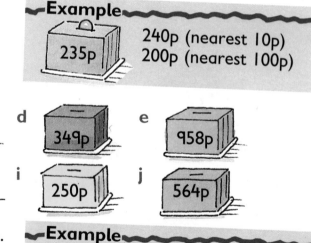

235p   240p (nearest 10p)
200p (nearest 100p)

1 Round the savings to the nearest 10p.
Now round them to the nearest 100p.

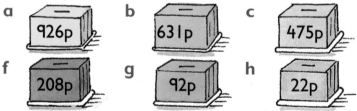

a 926p   b 631p   c 475p   d 349p   e 958p

f 208p   g 92p   h 22p   i 250p   j 564p

2 Round the prices on the toys to the nearest 10p.
Now round them to the nearest £.

Example

£3·56   £3·60 (nearest 10p)
£4 (nearest £)

a £4·82   b FIRE £6·47   c £9·15   d £19·99

e £16·55   f £1·06   g £2·50   h £6·59

6

Estimating all

Refresher

1 Round the red numbers to the nearest 10.

| 70 | 80 | 90 | 100 | 110 | 120 | 130 | 140 |

77   85   94   106   115   122   135

2 Round the green numbers to the nearest 10.

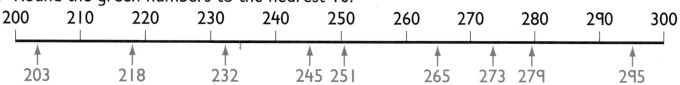

| 200 | 210 | 220 | 230 | 240 | 250 | 260 | 270 | 280 | 290 | 300 |

203   218   232   245 251   265   273 279   295

3 Now round the green numbers to the nearest 100.

Practice

1 Estimate the height of each person to the nearest centimetre.
Now estimate their height to the nearest 10 cm.

a

cm 129 128 127 126 125

b
cm 152 151 150 149 148

c
cm 161 160 159

d
cm 220 210 200

2 Round the distances to the nearest 10 km.
Now round them to the nearest 100 km.

a ⟨ 253 km

b ⟨ 176 km

c ⟨ 345 km

d ⟨ 497 km

3 Measure each line to the nearest centimetre.

a ————————————————

b ——————

c ——————————————

d ————————————————

Diamond numbers

Write four addition or subtraction calculations to make the
number on the diamond.

Refresher

 29

 37

 45

 34

Practice

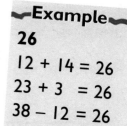

 65

 78

 59

 86

 93

 76

 78

Double trouble

Work out the calculations using a double
that you know to help you.
Write down the double you used.

Remember to
use your doubles!

Refresher

a $8 + 9 =$ ☐

b $11 + 10 =$ ☐

c $12 + 11 =$ ☐

d $13 + 14 =$ ☐

e $22 + 21 =$ ☐

f $18 + 21 =$ ☐

g $31 + 30 =$ ☐

h $42 + 41 =$ ☐

i $27 + 24 =$ ☐

j $39 + 38 =$ ☐

k $52 + 51 =$ ☐

Practice

a $47 + 46 =$ ☐

b $63 + 64 =$ ☐

c $74 + 72 =$ ☐

d $81 + 84 =$ ☐

e $93 + 94 =$ ☐

f $107 + 108 =$ ☐

g $130 + 120 =$ ☐

h $124 + 123 =$ ☐

i $155 + 160 =$ ☐

j $172 + 174 =$ ☐

k $180 + 190 =$ ☐

l $162 + 159 =$ ☐

Leaping along

Refresher

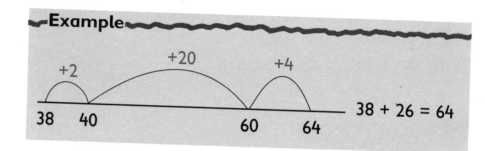

Example

$$38 + 26 = 64$$

I These calculations have been worked out using an empty number line.

Draw the number lines and the jumps. Then label all the jumps.

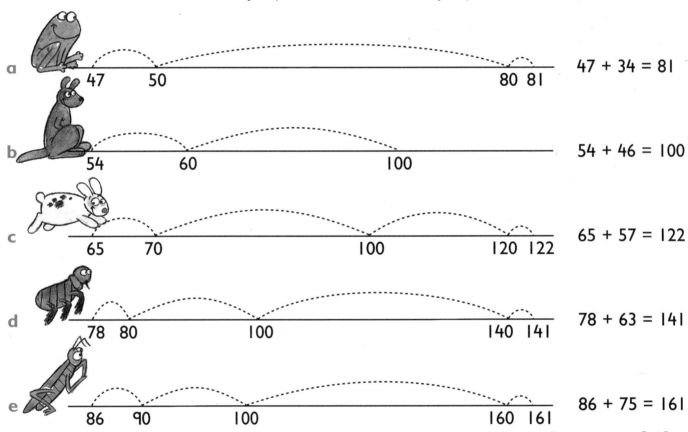

a 47 + 34 = 81

b 54 + 46 = 100

c 65 + 57 = 122

d 78 + 63 = 141

e 86 + 75 = 161

Practice

I Work out these calculations using an empty number line.

a 67 + 53 = ☐	b 88 + 73 = ☐	c 129 + 57 = ☐
d 136 + 9 = ☐	e 151 + 89 = ☐	f 196 + 76 = ☐
g 137 + 149 = ☐	h 163 + 178 = ☐	i 186 + 228 = ☐
j 177 + 209 = ☐	k 264 + 279 = ☐	l 378 + 413 = ☐
m 425 + 318 = ☐	n 566 + 437 = ☐	o 265 + 578 = ☐

Baking additions

Write these calculations out vertically, then add the hundreds, tens and units.

Refresher

 a 52 + 37

 b 35 + 64

 c 74 + 21

d 63 + 32

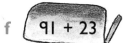 e 46 + 59

f 91 + 23

g 59 + 33

h 75 + 58

i 94 + 87

Practice

 a 168 + 75

 b 265 + 63

 c 279 + 52

 d 381 + 49

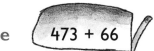 e 473 + 66

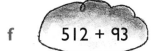 f 512 + 93

 g 286 + 196

h 219 + 286

 i 345 + 267

j 462 + 499

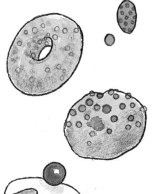

Fruit tree addition

Refresher

Choose one number from the apple tree and one from the pear tree to make 10 addition calculations. Round the number from the pear tree up to 100.

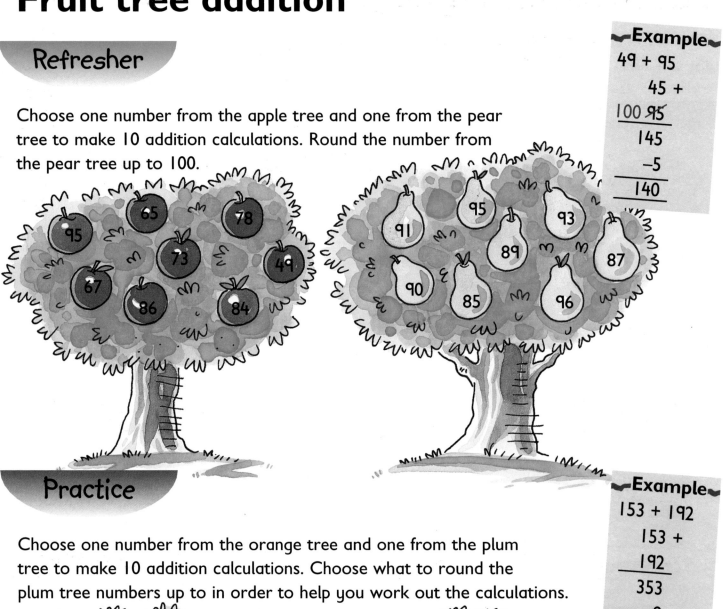

Example

49 + 95

  45 +
$$\underline{100 \ 95}$$
145
 −5
$$\overline{140}$$

Practice

Choose one number from the orange tree and one from the plum tree to make 10 addition calculations. Choose what to round the plum tree numbers up to in order to help you work out the calculations.

Example

153 + 192

 153 +
$$\underline{192}$$
353
 −8
$$\overline{345}$$

12

Subtraction highlights

Work out the subtraction calculations, using an empty number line or the vertical method.

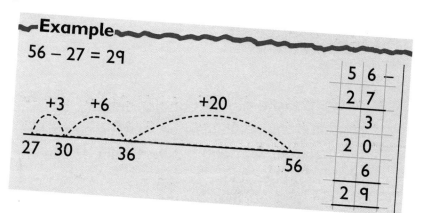

Example

56 − 27 = 29

Refresher

a 58 − 34 = ☐

b 82 − 43 = ☐

c 78 − 39 = ☐

d 67 − 24 = ☐

e 56 − 32 = ☐

f 49 − 23 = ☐

g 74 − 51 = ☐

h 86 − 27 = ☐

i 94 − 57 = ☐

Practice

a 176 − 53 = ☐

b 159 − 67 = ☐

c 164 − 94 = ☐

d 187 − 62 = ☐

e 247 − 78 = ☐

f 254 − 147 = ☐

g 372 − 235 = ☐

h 456 − 251 = ☐

i 438 − 212 = ☐

j 396 − 231 = ☐

k 539 − 368 = ☐

l 387 − 142 = ☐

Subtraction round-up

Refresher

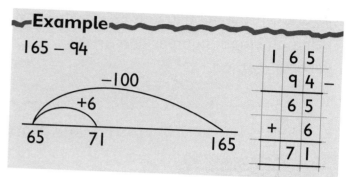

Example

165 – 94

1 Work out the subtraction calculations by rounding the number to be subtracted to 100. Record your working out vertically or use an empty number line.

a 148 – 96 = ☐   b 159 – 98 = ☐   c 176 – 91 = ☐   d 183 – 90 = ☐

e 164 – 89 = ☐   f 178 – 87 = ☐   g 245 – 85 = ☐   h 239 – 88 = ☐

i 239 – 88 = ☐   j 267 – 80 = ☐   k 256 – 81 = ☐   l 279 – 94 = ☐

Practice

1 Work out these calculations. Round the number to be subtracted to the next multiple of 10 or 100. Record your working out vertically or use an empty number line.

a 354 – 89 = ☐   b 476 – 85 = ☐   c 562 – 197 = ☐   d 637 – 284 = ☐

e 519 – 192 = ☐   f 637 – 292 = ☐   g 345 – 198 = ☐   h 533 – 249 = ☐

i 297 – 78 = ☐   j 436 – 167 = ☐   k 525 – 178 = ☐   l 326 – 177 = ☐

Count your money

Refresher

1   Work out the value of the coins in each row and
    record the amount in pounds and pence.

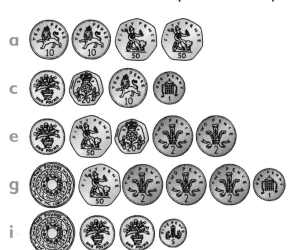

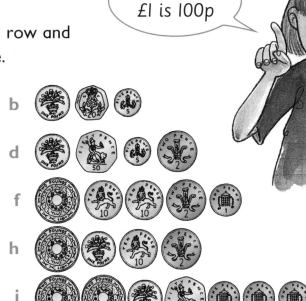

Remember
£1 is 100p

Practice

Convert it!

A game for 2 players

You will need: 10 different-coloured counters for each player

How to play:

● Take turns to point to a square on the grid.

● Your partner has to convert that amount
  into pounds and pence and explain how
  they worked it out.

● If their answer is right, they put one of
  their counters on that square.

● When all the grid is covered, the player
  with the most counters on it is the winner.

524p
is £5·24

524p	693p	744p	1025p	1497p
1526p	1755p	1964p	2004p	2617p
2351p	2784p	2615p	3185p	3851p
3008p	3999p	2732p	1611p	2222p

Fairground problems

Merry-go-round
£1·35

Dodgems
£2·20

Big Wheel
£2·85

Use the prices to work out the answers to the problems.
When you have finished, make up some questions for a friend.

Hamburger
£1·80

Refresher

a Sally has £2 to spend. What ride can she go on and
how much change will she get?

b Ben rides on the merry-go-round and the dodgems.
How much does he spend?

c Mary buys a small drink and a toffee apple. How
much does she spend?

d Jake has £5 to spend. He buys a hamburger. How
much does he have left?

e Theo wants to have one turn on each of the rides.
How much money will he need?

Small Cola
90p

Large Cola
£1·15

8°COLA

Practice

a Grace has a ride on the big wheel and then gets a hamburger.
How much does she spend?

b Nick wants two rides on the dodgems and pays with a £10 note.
What will his change be?

c Max and Amy each have a ride on the dodgems and then on the
big wheel. How much have they both spent altogether?

d Steve buys a small drink for himself and a large drink for his dad.
He pays with a £20 note. How much change will he get?

e Tim has two rides at the fair. He spent £3·55.
What were the two rides?

Toffee apple
75p

Library problems

Find the answers to each problem.

Refresher

  a In the science section there are 68 books on the top shelf and 74 books on the bottom shelf. How many science books are there altogether?

  b There are 124 picture books in the children's library. On Monday, 95 were taken out. How many were left?

  c Two classes of children visited the library. The first class took out 37 books and the second class took out 45 books. How many books were taken out altogether?

  d On Monday 34 cookery books were taken out, on Tuesday 56 and on Wednesday 18. How many were taken out altogether?

  e There are 148 sports books. 59 got ruined in a flood. How many were left undamaged?

Practice

  a In the reference library there are 88 books on the top shelf, 112 on the middle shelf and 145 on the bottom shelf. How many reference books altogether?

  b Two classes of children visited the library on Thursday. Altogether they returned 121 books. The first class returned 65 books. How many did the second class return?

  c 127 books were returned on Friday morning, 239 in the afternoon. The total returns for the day was 557. How many were returned in the evening?

  d The art section of the library contains 402 books. There are 134 on the top shelf, 161 on the middle shelf. How many are on the bottom shelf?

  e In the history section there are 184 books on the top shelf , 87 on the bottom shelf. The librarian removes 72 of the books. How many are left?

Measuring straws

Refresher

1 Draw lines of these lengths.

a 10 mm   b 90 mm

c 35 mm   d 65 mm

e 45 mm   f 55 mm

g 95 mm   h 5 mm

Measure from the zero mark on your ruler

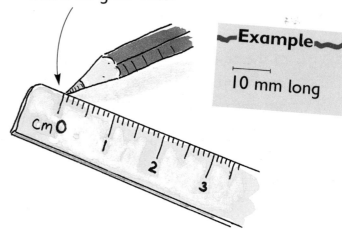

~Example~

10 mm long

Practice

1 Measure each straw in millimetres, then draw a line of the same length.

Underneath the line, write the length in three different ways.

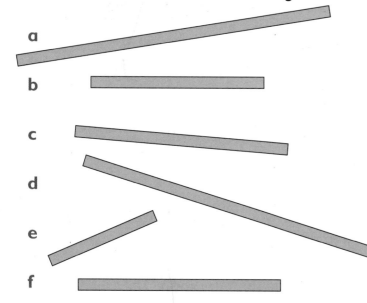

a

b

c

d

e

f

g

~Example~

7 cm 4 mm or $7\frac{4}{10}$ cm or 74 mm

2 Draw lines of these lengths.

a 3 cm shorter than 74 mm   b 2 cm longer than 47 mm

c 4 cm shorter than 58 mm   d 5 cm longer than 100 mm

Centimetre carpets

Refresher

1 Write down the lengths shown on this measuring tape in decimal form.

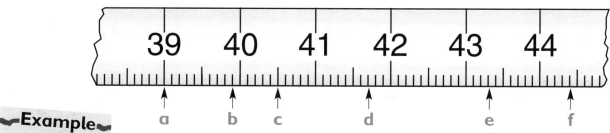

| 39 | 40 | 41 | 42 | 43 | 44 |

a   b   c   d   e   f

Example

b = 39·9 cm

Practice

is the same length as

←——————→

1 Look at each measurement and write its equivalent in metres or centimetres.

a 425 cm   ←——→   <u>4 m 25 cm</u>   b 137 cm   ←——→   _____

c 5 m 60 cm   ←——→   _____   d 64 cm   ←——→   _____

e 3 m 8 cm   ←——→   _____   f $8\frac{63}{100}$ m   ←——→   _____

g $2\frac{40}{100}$ m   ←——→   _____   h $\frac{24}{100}$ m   ←——→   _____

i $2\frac{4}{100}$ m   ←——→   _____   j $\frac{25}{100}$ m   ←——→   _____

2 Jean is fitting carpets in a new hotel.
She has these rolls of identical carpet.

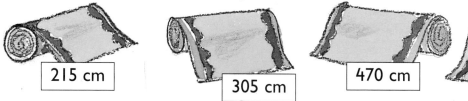

215 cm   305 cm   470 cm   525 cm

RUSTEAN Carpets

Write, in metres, the different lengths of carpet she can make by fitting together any 2 rolls.

Jogging in metres

Refresher

1 Write these lengths as a fraction of a metre.

   a 10 cm   b 50 cm   c 25 cm

   d 75 cm   e 100 mm   f 500 mm

   g 250 mm   h 750 mm

   Remember:
   $10\,cm = \frac{1}{10}\,m.$

2 Copy and complete this table by writing in the equivalent measurements in millimetres, centimetres or metres.

mm	cm	m
100 mm	10 cm	$\frac{1}{10}$ m
200 mm	_____ cm	$\frac{2}{10}$ m
_____ mm	30 cm	_____ m
_____ mm	_____ cm	$\frac{6}{10}$ m

Practice

is the same as ⟷

1 Look at this three-way relationship. Draw a triangle relationship for the measurements below.

   a 400 mm   b 50 cm   c $\frac{7}{10}$ m

   d 250 mm   e 90 cm   f $\frac{3}{4}$ m

300 mm

30 cm $\frac{3}{10}$ m

2 Copy and complete this table by writing in the equivalent measurements in millimetres, centimetres or metres.

km	m
$\frac{1}{2}$ km	500 m
$\frac{1}{4}$ km	_____ m
_____ km	100 m
$\frac{3}{4}$ km	_____ m
$\frac{7}{10}$ km	_____ m
_____ km	900 m

3 Put these distances in order, starting with the smallest.

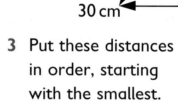

960 m
1·0 km
$\frac{3}{4}$ km
906 m
$1\frac{1}{4}$ km
$\frac{9}{10}$ km
1 km 100 m

20

Measurement round up

Refresher

1 Round these lengths to the nearest 10 cm.

a 456 cm ⟶ 460 cm

b 465 cm

c 546 cm

d 564 cm

e 654 cm

f 645 cm

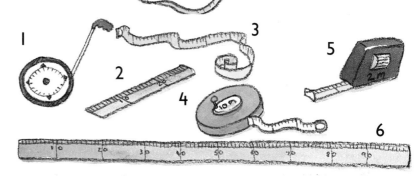

Practice

These are some of the tools you can use to measure length. Work with a partner to measure things what have a length between 1 and 10 metres.

1 a Copy the table. In the first column, write what you are going to measure. In the next column, write the number of the measuring tool you are going to use.

b Measure to the nearest centimetre. Record the actual length in two ways, then round it to the nearest 10 cm.

2 Now choose two more things to measure and record your answers.

What we measured	Tool	Actual length m/cm	m	Rounded to the nearest 10 cm
1 length of window sill	4	6m 43cm	6·43m	640cm
2 width of				
3 depth of				
4 height of				
5 distance to…from…				
6				
7				

Add your own ideas here.

21

Fun run

Refresher

1 Look at the race course then copy and complete this table, writing the distances in metres and kilometres.

	Distance	
	m	**km**
Sports centre to school	500m	$\frac{1}{2}$ km
School to library		
Library to sports centre		
Sports centre to farm		
Farm to church		

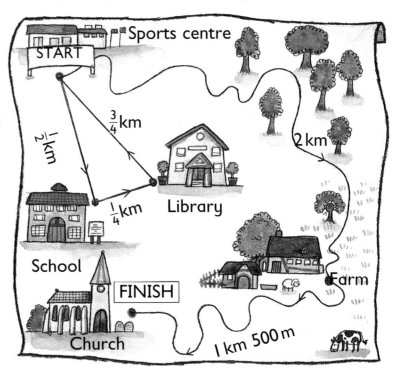

Practice

Six children have entered a 5 km fun run. Coming up to the finishing line, they are in these positions.

Andrew	200 m from the finishing line
Bola	$\frac{1}{10}$ km behind Andrew
Clare	$\frac{2}{10}$ ahead of Bola
Deepak	400 m behind Clare
Ella	$\frac{1}{2}$ km behind Andrew
David	300 m ahead of Ella

1 Draw a line and mark the position of each runner on the line.

$\frac{7}{10}$km $\frac{6}{10}$km $\frac{5}{10}$km $\frac{4}{10}$km $\frac{3}{10}$km $\frac{2}{10}$km $\frac{1}{10}$km

Andrew ↓   Finish

2 What is the distance in metres between:
   a Clare and Andrew   b Bola and Ella   c David and Bola   d Clare and David

3 a Which two runners are furthest apart?   b What is the distance between them?

4 a How many kilometres has Deepak run?   b How far has Deepak still to run?

Pinboard perimeters

Refresher

1 Make these rectangles on your pinboard.
2 Count the number of units around the edge to find the perimeter.

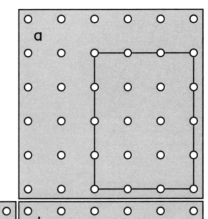

Example
4 + 3 + 4 + 3
is 14 units

Practice

1 Use your pinboard to find the following and record each one on 1 cm dot paper.
   a 2 rectangles with a perimeter of 12 units
   b 3 rectangles with a perimeter of 18 units
2 a Make these shapes with 5 cubes.

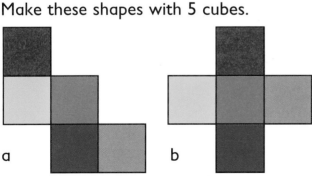

a

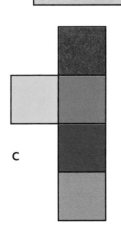

b

c

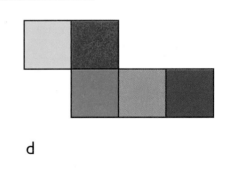

d

   b Find the perimeter of each shape.
3 a Make different shapes with 5 cubes.
   b Draw each shape on 1 cm dot paper and find its perimeter in centimetres.
   c Colour the shapes that have the same perimeter.

23

Try out triangles

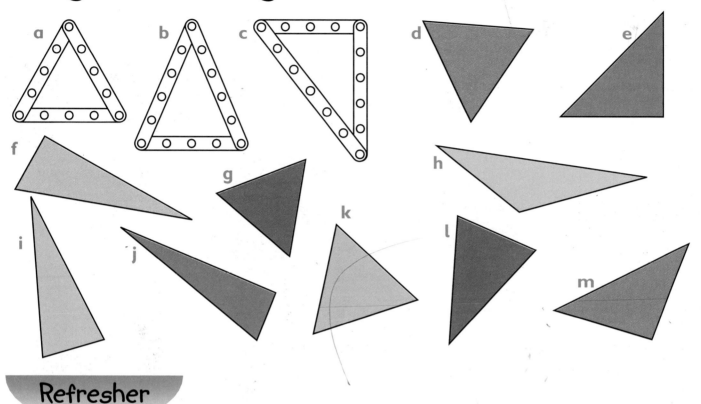

Refresher

1 Make triangles **a**, **b** and **c** with geostrips. Label them equilateral, isosceles or right-angled.

2 Find three more triangles, one of each type. Write down its letter and name.

Practice

1 **a** Copy the table and sort the triangles in three ways.

Equilateral	Isosceles	Other
a,		

b In the last column, circle the letters which represent right-angled triangles.

2 **a** Take a square of paper and fold it diagonally, and then diagonally again.

b Cut out the 4 triangles.

c Use all 4 triangles to make a large isosceles triangle.

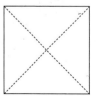

Shape investigation

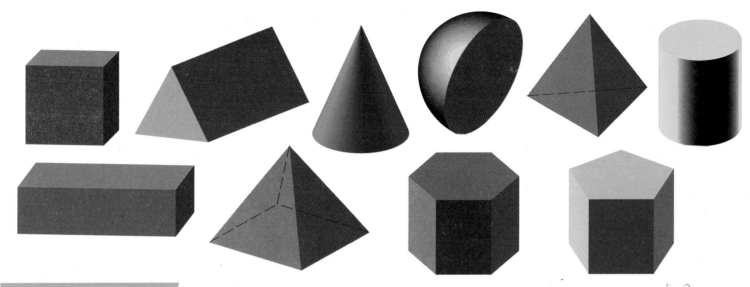

Refresher

I Sherlock Holmes is hunting for shapes. The table shows the properties he is looking for. Copy and complete the table.

Shape	Is a prism	Has triangular faces	Has 8 vertices
cube	✓	✗	✓

Practice

The case of the missing shapes
Description:
The number of the edges of an end face is 2 less than the total number of faces of a prism.

I Draw up a table like this. Name the shapes above and write down their properties.

Shape	Is a prism	Number of faces	Number of edges of an end face
cube	✓	6	4

25

Proper polygons

Refresher

You will need: a set of 2D shapes

I Use the diagrams to sort your set of 2D shapes.

a
Regular	Irregular

b
Has line symmetry	Has no line symmetry

c
Has a right angle	Has no right angles

Practice

I Use the diagrams to sort your set of 2D shapes.

a
	Triangles	Quadrilaterals
regular		
irregular		

b
	Regular	Irregular
has line symmetry		
has no line symmetry		

c Now choose your own criteria and sort your shapes in a different way.

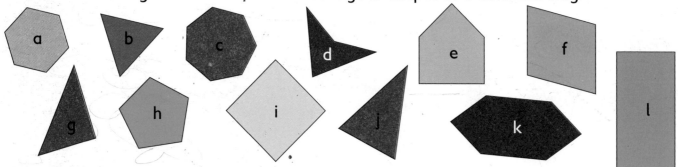

2 Copy and complete the table for the above shapes.

Property	Shape
all sides equal	
2 or more right angles	
more than 1 line of symmetry	

Co-ordinates treasure hunt

Refresher

1 The map shows where the pirates are digging for treasure. Dick is digging at the point (4, 3). Write the co-ordinates for the other pirates in the same way.

Abe (2,   )
Zack
Greg
Jack
Mick

2 Captain Black is digging at a position between Zack and Greg. What might the co-ordinates be?

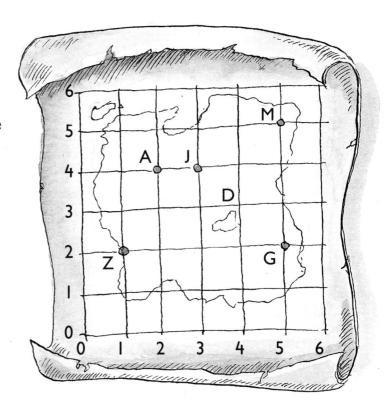

Practice

1 Captain Black's map has a secret code. Read the co-ordinates to find out where the treasure is buried. Each line is a new word.

(4, 4) (4, 2) (4, 5)
(1, 4) (1, 1) (3, 1) (5, 1) (4, 4)
(1, 2) (3, 4) (5, 3) (3, 3)
(5, 4) (3, 2) (5, 1)
(3, 1) (1, 1) (2, 5) (5, 1)

2 Use the co-ordinates in question 1.
a Write your first name.
b Write where you think the treasure is buried, then ask a friend to read it.

27

Postcard area

You will need: a supply of squares, rectangles, circles, coins, cubes

Refresher

1 Cover the postcard with shapes of the same size. Choose three different covering units.

Example
12 circles cover the postcard.

Practice

1 Write down the number of 1 cm cubes you use to cover the surface of each of shape.

a   b   c   d

a __6__ cubes   b ____ cubes   c ____ cubes   d ____ cubes

2 Copy and complete.

a Shape **a** is _____ cubes smaller than shape **d**.

b Shape _____ is 2 cubes larger than shape _____.

3 Count the number of small squares in each shape to find its area.

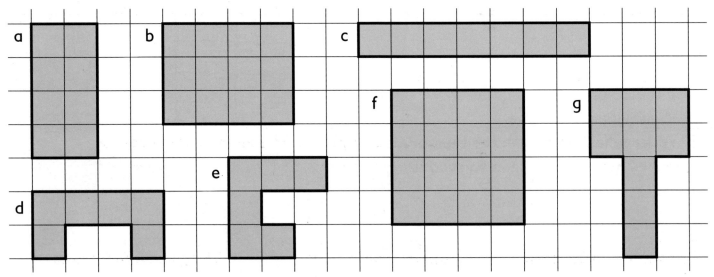

Dotty shapes

Refresher

1   Find the areas of these pinboard shapes.

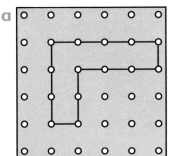
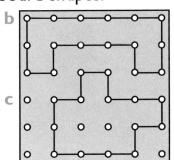

Practice

1   Draw these rectangles on 1 cm squared paper.
   Below each one write its area.

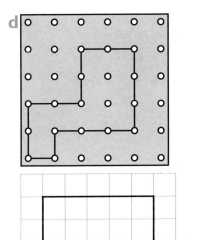

area = 15 square centimetres

   a 5 cm long and 3 cm wide

   b 4 cm long and 3 cm wide

   c 7 cm long and 5 cm wide

   d 10 cm long and 2 cm wide

2   Draw these shapes on 1 cm squared paper.

   a $5\frac{1}{2}$ square centimetres

   b $7\frac{1}{2}$ square centimetres

   c $9\frac{1}{2}$ square centimetres

   d 16 square centimetres

3   You can only see part of these rectangles and shapes.
   The area of each rectangle and shape is shown. Copy and complete each one.

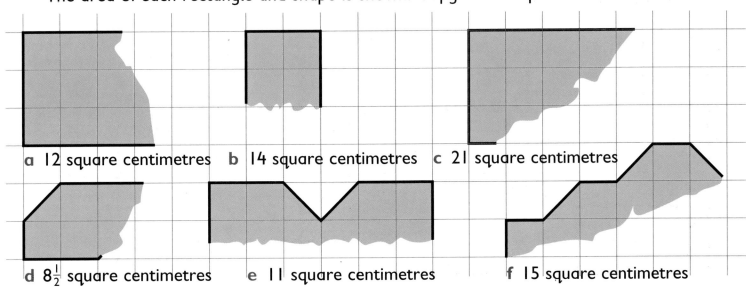

a 12 square centimetres   b 14 square centimetres   c 21 square centimetres

d $8\frac{1}{2}$ square centimetres   e 11 square centimetres   f 15 square centimetres

● Measure and calculate the area of rectangles and other simple shapes, using counting methods and standard units (cm, cm²)

Au 6, 3

Shape measurement

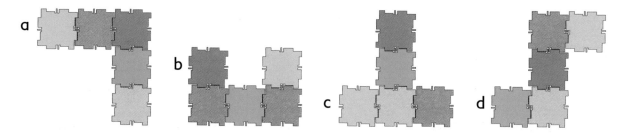

Refresher

1 a Make these shapes with interlocking squares.

a

b

c

d

b Draw each shape on squared paper and find its area and perimeter.

Practice

1 a Make pentomino jigsaws using interlocking squares. Draw each shape on squared paper. Use colour to show how the pentominoes fit together.

   b Record the area and perimeter of each shape.

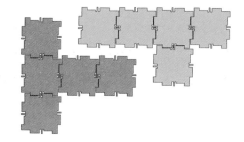

2 a Make a rectangle 5 units by 3 units with these three pentominoes.

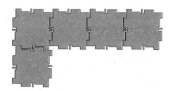 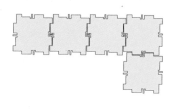 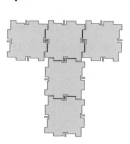

   b Make a rectangle 5 units by 4 units with these four pentominoes.

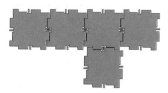 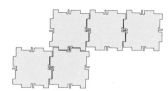  

30

Travel numbers

Refresher

1 Copy and complete the number sequences.

   a 11, 13, 15, 17, __, __, 23, 25, __, __   b 12, 16, 20, __, 28, 32, __, __, __, __

   c 1, 5, 9, 13, __, __, __, __, __, __   d 59, 61, 63, __, __, __, __, __, 75, __

   e 44, 40, __, __, __, 24, __, 16, __, __

2 Add 2 to each of these numbers.

   a 82   b 56   c 97

   d 31   e 100   f 75

3 Add 4 to each of these numbers.

   a 30   b 27   c 56

   d 85   e 96   f 34

Practice

1 These buses started their journey with the number of people shown on each bus.
   They picked up 4 people at every bus stop. Write how many people are
   on each bus after each stop. The bus is full after 10 stops.

a Start at 1. Add 4 each time.	b Start at 2. Add 4 each time.	c Start at 3. Add 4 each time.	d Start at 4. Add 4 each time.
1 5	2	3	4 ... ...

2 Look carefully at the units digits in each list. Write them out.

   a What patterns can you see?

   b What patterns are the same?

   c What patterns are different?

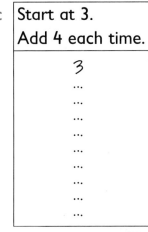

─Example─
a 1, 5, ..., ..., ..., ...
b 2, ..., ..., ..., ..., ...
c 3, ..., ..., ..., ..., ...
d 4, ..., ..., ..., ..., ...

Step multiples

Refresher

1 Climb each set of steps by counting in multiples of 25, 50 or 100.

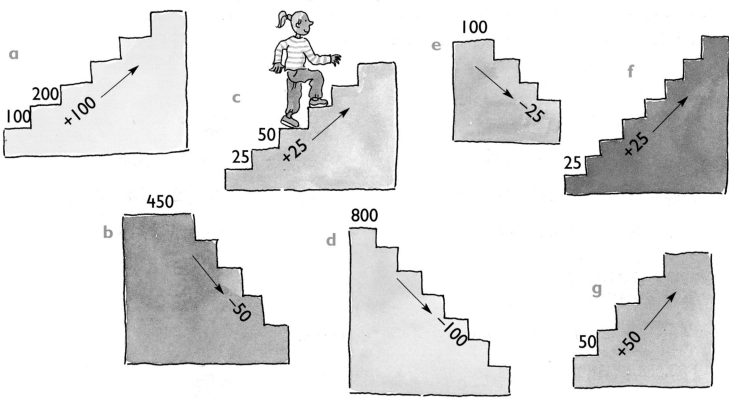

Practice

1 Write down the multiple of 25 that **comes before** these numbers.

    a 100   b 350   c 500

    d 275   e 425   f 150

2 Write the multiple of 25 that **comes after** these numbers.

    a 50   b 275   c 450

    d 400   e 325   f 150

3 a Write 4 multiples of 25.
  b Write 4 multiples of 25 between 300 and 500.
  c Write 4 multiples of 25 less than 200.
  d Write 4 multiples of 25 that are also multiples of 50.
  e Write 4 multiples of 25 that are also multiples of 100.
  f Write 3 multiples of 25 that add up to 175.
  g Write 3 multiples of 25 that add up to more than 200.

Odd or even?

Refresher

1 The number cards are in odd and even groups. One number in each group of cards is incorrect. Copy the numbers and change the incorrect number. Decide whether the number group is odd or even.

a 78 80 8̶1̶ (82) 84 86 → even

b 766 764 761 760 758 → ____

c 125 127 129 131 134 → ____

d 911 913 915 916 919 → ____

e 263 265 268 269 271 → ____

f 555 553 552 549 547 → ____

g 300 298 296 294 295 → ____

h 199 200 203 205 207 → ____

i 401 402 404 406 408 → ____

j 888 886 884 883 880 → ____

Practice

1 Write a series of numbers to match these statements.

a The units digits of even numbers are 0, 2, 4 6, 8.

b After 1 every second number is odd.

c The units digits of odd numbers are 1, 3, 5, 7, 9.

d The numbers on both sides of odd numbers are even.

e The sum of two even numbers is even.

f The sum of 2 odd numbers is even.

2 Which one of these statements is true?

Even + even + even = even

Odd + odd + odd = even

33

Jigsaw numbers

1 2 3 4 5 6 7 8 9 10

Refresher

1 Add these consecutive numbers.

a   3 + 4 = ☐

b   7 + 8 = ☐

c   5 + 6 + 7 = ☐

d   6 + 7 + 8 = ☐

e   8 + 9 + ~~19~~ = ☐
                10

f   3 + 4 + 5 + 6 = ☐

g   5 + 6 + 7 + 8 = ☐

h   7 + 8 + 9 + 10 = ☐

i   2 + 3 + 4 + 5 + 6 = ☐

j   5 + 6 + 7 + 8 + 9 = ☐

Practice

4 + 5 = 9
2 + 3 + 4 = 9
The consecutive numbers add to make the total 9.

1
● Write the numbers 1 to 20.

● Try to find consecutive numbers that add together to make each of the numbers 1 to 20.

● Is it possible?
1 = ?
2 = ?
3 = 1 + 2
4 = ?
5 = 2 + 3
....

2
● Write the numbers 1 to 20, as in question 1.

● Find all of the numbers that can be made by adding 2 consecutive numbers.

● Find all of the numbers that can be made by adding 3 consecutive numbers.

● Write down any patterns you found.

34

Number order

Refresher

- Using each number card once only, make some 3-digit numbers.
- Write the numbers you have made in order, starting with the smallest.
- Repeat four more times.

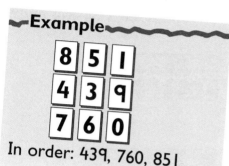

Example

8	5	1
4	3	9
7	6	0

In order: 439, 760, 851

Practice

Use the number cards 1–10 to make 3-digit numbers.

1
- Using each card once only, make the three largest numbers possible and write them down.
- Now make the three smallest numbers possible and write them down.

2 You may use each card again in a different number.
Make ten even numbers and write them down. Now write them again in order, starting with the smallest.
This time make ten odd numbers and write them down.
Write the numbers in order, starting with the smallest.

3 Using each card once only:
- Make five multiples of 5.
- Make five multiples of 10.
- Make five multiples of 25.
- Make five multiples of 50.

4 You may use each card again in a different number.
- Using consecutive numbers, make as many 3-digit numbers as you can.
- Write the numbers down in order, starting with the largest.

35

Multiplication scores

Refresher

1 Write two matching multiplication facts and addition facts.

a    b 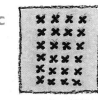   c    d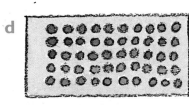

$3 \times 4 = 12$
$4 + 4 + 4 = 12$
$4 \times 3 = 12$
$3 + 3 + 3 + 3 = 12$

f    g    h

e

Example

$3 \times 2 = \boxed{}$ $8 \times 3 = \boxed{}$

$5 \times 10 = \boxed{}$

Practice

1 Follow the rules to calculate the score for each dart thrown.

a 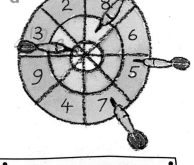   b 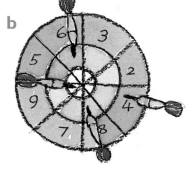   c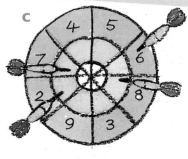

Darts Rules

White:	× 2
Yellow:	× 3
Green:	× 10

Darts Rules

White:	× 5
Yellow:	× 4
Green:	× 2

Darts Rules

White:	× 3
Yellow:	× 4
Green:	× 5

2 Copy and complete the multiplication calculations.

a $4 \times 5 = \boxed{}$ $6 \times 3 = \boxed{}$ $7 \times 2 = \boxed{}$ $8 \times 10 = \boxed{}$ $5 \times 5 = \boxed{}$

b $8 \times 4 = \boxed{}$ $9 \times 3 = \boxed{}$ $8 \times 2 = \boxed{}$ $7 \times 5 = \boxed{}$ $10 \times 10 = \boxed{}$

c $\boxed{} \times 3 = 21$ $\boxed{} \times 4 = 24$ $4 \times \boxed{} = 32$ $5 \times \boxed{} = 40$ $\boxed{} \times 8 = 16$

Sweet facts

Refresher

1 Write two multiplication and two division facts for each picture.

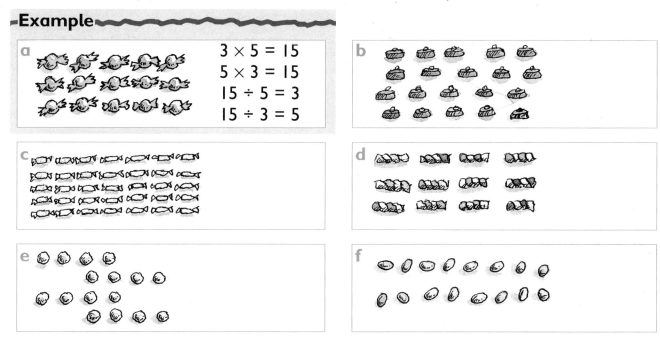

Example

a
$3 \times 5 = 15$
$5 \times 3 = 15$
$15 \div 5 = 3$
$15 \div 3 = 5$

b

c

d

e

f

Practice

1 Write a division fact to show how many pieces of chocolate are in each row.
Write the multiplication fact you can use to check your answer.

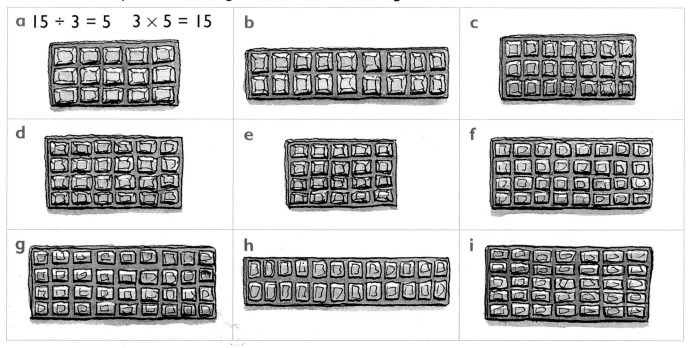

a $15 \div 3 = 5$ $3 \times 5 = 15$

b

c

d

e

f

g

h

i

● Derive quickly doubles of all whole numbers to 50
● Approximates first: use informal pencil and paper methods ...

Au 8, 3

Starry doubles

Refresher

Example

20 + 20 = 40
2 × 20 = 40

1 Double all of the numbers below.
   Write an addition and multiplication fact for each.

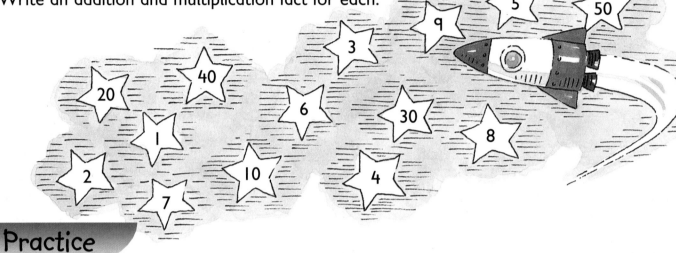

Practice

1 Write the multiples of 10 that each star number is between.
   Decide which multiple of 10 the star number is closest to and circle it.

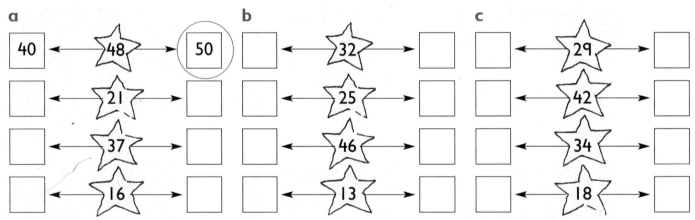

2 Give an approximate answer to the multiplication
   calculations. Now work out each answer, using
   the grid method.

Example

48 × 3 → (50 × 3 = 150)

	40	8	
× 3	120	24	= 144

   a 24 × 3   b 36 × 4   c 45 × 3   d 19 × 4

   e 37 × 2   f 49 × 3   g 16 × 5   h 25 × 5

   i 46 × 2   j 34 × 4   k 23 × 5   l 18 × 4

Sports score division

Refresher

1   Write an approximate answer to each division calculation.

a 26 ÷ 2   b 69 ÷ 3

c 88 ÷ 4   d 46 ÷ 2

e 55 ÷ 5   f 66 ÷ 3

g 48 ÷ 4   h 64 ÷ 2

i 84 ÷ 2   j 96 ÷ 3

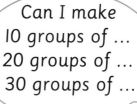

Can I make
10 groups of ...
20 groups of ...
30 groups of ...

Practice

1   The scores are all wrong. Follow the instructions at the
beginning of each row to work out the correct scores.

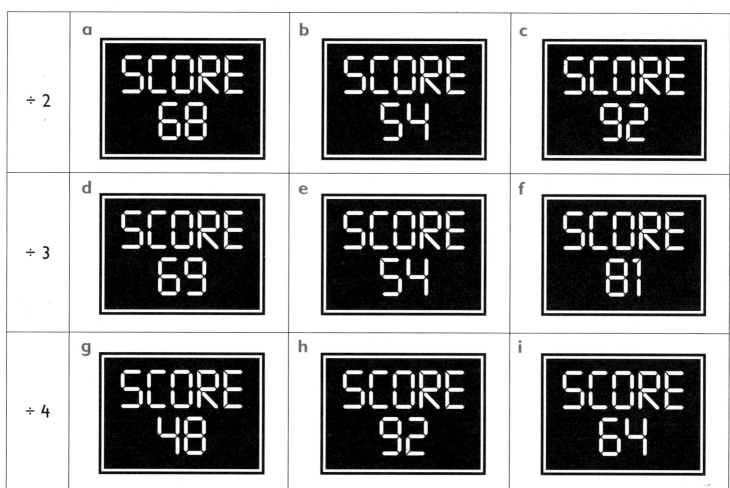

	a	b	c
÷ 2	SCORE 68	SCORE 54	SCORE 92
÷ 3	SCORE 69	SCORE 54	SCORE 81
÷ 4	SCORE 48	SCORE 92	SCORE 64

A question of sport

Refresher

I Decide which operation you would use to answer each problem.

a Goggles cost ⬚?. Mike buys ⬚? pairs. How much does he spend?

c Sarah buys a swimming cap and a kickboard. How much does she spend ⬚?

e Mrs Ryan has £⬚?. She pays £⬚? to go swimming. How much change does she get?

b It cost ⬚? for ⬚? children to enter the pool. How much did it cost each child?

d A box of swimming caps costs ⬚?. Each cap costs ⬚?. How many caps in a box?

f Kickboards cost ⬚? each. How much does it cost for ⬚??

Practice

I Decide which operation you will use to answer each problem. Now calculate the answer.

a How much does it cost to hire each item for a full day?

b There are 6 people in the Kelly family. They all hire a pair of boots for the day. How much does it cost altogether?

c There are 8 children in the ski school group. Each child hires boots and skis for half a day. What is the cost for each child? What is the cost for the whole group?

d Mum, Dad and 2 children go skiing for 1 day. They each hire boots, skis and poles. What is the total cost? What is the total cost for 2 days?

e Jim has £80. How many full days can he ski for? How many half days can he ski for?

f My friend hires a snowboard for 3 days. What is the total cost?

g The total cost for 2 people to hire goods from the shop for 1 day was £36. What did they hire?

Fast 5s

Refresher

1 Multiply the number shown on each calculator by 10. Write the new number.

Example
$17 \times 10 = 170$

a  15

b  8

c  12

d  30

e  14

f 9

g 20

h 16

i 10

j 19

Practice

1 Use the rule shown on the notebook to find the answers to these calculations.

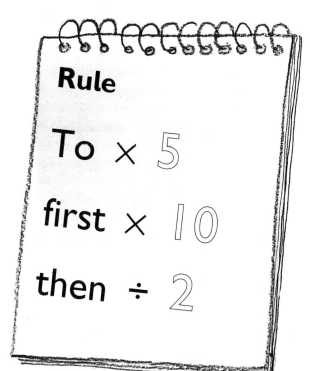

Rule

To × 5

first × 10

then ÷ 2

Example
$(16 \times 10) \div 2$
$= 160 \div 2 = 80$

a 16×5 ⟶

b 11×5

c 20×5

d 19×5

e 30×5

f 12×5

g 40×5

h 18×5

i 50×5

j 15×5

2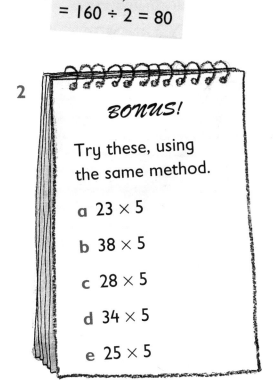

BONUS!

Try these, using the same method.

a 23×5

b 38×5

c 28×5

d 34×5

e 25×5

Speedy 20s

Refresher

1 Double each of the numbers below.

a

b

Practice

1 Use the rule on the notebook to find the answers
to these calculations.

Rule

To × 20

first × 10

then × 2

a 14 × 20 ⟶

b 11 × 20

c 16 × 20

d 20 × 20

e 13 × 20

f 15 × 20

g 30 × 20

h 12 × 20

i 18 × 20

j 19 × 20

Example

$(14 \times 10) \times 2$
$= 140 \times 2 = 280$

2

BONUS!

Try these, using
the same method.

a 50 × 20

b 24 × 20

c 32 × 20

d 21 × 20

e 42 × 20

Easy eights

Refresher

1 Find all the multiples of 4 in the treasure chest.
Now write out the number fact for each multiple.

Practice

2 a Complete each number fact for 4.
  b Look inside each card to find a fact for 8.
    Double your first answer to complete the fact for 8.

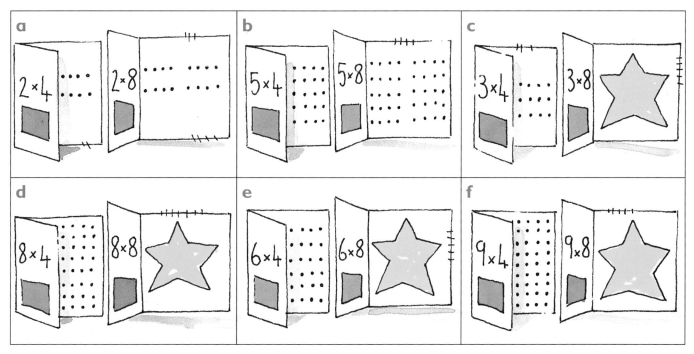

43

Chocolate egg fractions

1 Each of the big chocolate eggs has lots of tiny eggs inside. Split the big egg in half and share the small eggs with a friend. How many do you get each?

Example

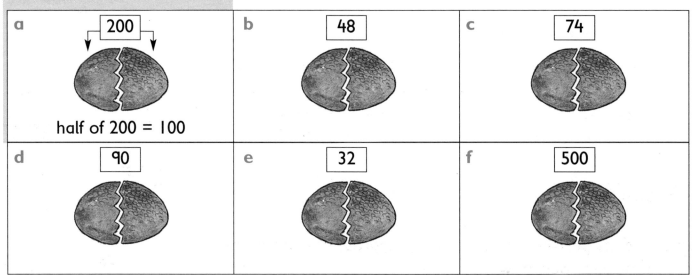

a **200**

half of 200 = 100

b **48**

c **74**

d **90**

e **32**

f **500**

1 Split the big egg into quarters and share the small eggs between 4 of you. How many do you get each?

Hint: find the answer by halving the first number, then halving again.

Example

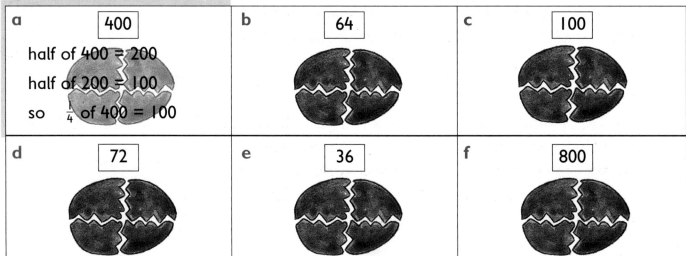

a **400**

half of 400 = 200

half of 200 = 100

so $\frac{1}{4}$ of 400 = 100

b **64**

c **100**

d **72**

e **36**

f **800**

● Use × and ÷ to solve word problems ... "real life" and money
● Choose and use appropriate number operations to solve problems

Au 9, 5

Musical maths

Refresher

1 Look at each problem. Work out the answer in your head and then write down the answer.

a Year 4 have enough money to buy 6 recorders. How much money do they have?	b John buys 2 flutes. How much does he spend?
c How much will it cost to have 4 hours of music lessons?	d Ali has only only saved half of the cost of the saxophone. How much has he saved?

Practice

1 Read the problems and choose an appropriate method of calculating your answer:

● mental ● mental with jottings ● pencil and paper

a Joey has enough money for 5 hours of music lessons. How much does he have?	b Recorders are packed in boxes of 7. How much does it cost to buy the box?
c The school buys 4 trumpets. What is the total cost?	d Megan buys a flute and a saxophone. She pays the total cost off over 4 weeks. How much does she pay each week?
e Mr Travis wants to buy 4 violins and 4 song sheets. He has £100. How much more does he need?	f Shamina gets £3 pocket money per week. How many weeks will it take her to save up for the saxophone?

saxophone £72

£8 recorder

£24 flute

£5

SONG SHEETS

£35

violin

£46

trumpet

MUSIC LESSONS £25 PER HOUR

Field fractions

Refresher

1 What fraction is one part of the field?

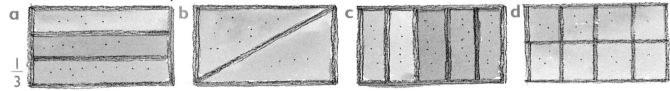

a $\frac{1}{3}$ b c d

Practice

1 Write down the fraction of the field that is planted.
Now write down the fraction that is not planted.

a $\frac{3}{4}$ $\frac{1}{4}$ b c d

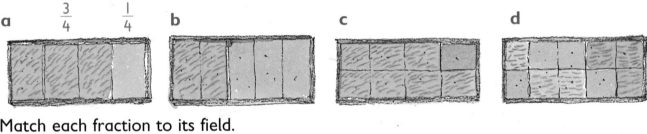

3 Match each fraction to its field.

$\frac{2}{3}$ $\frac{7}{8}$

$\frac{1}{2}$ $\frac{3}{4}$

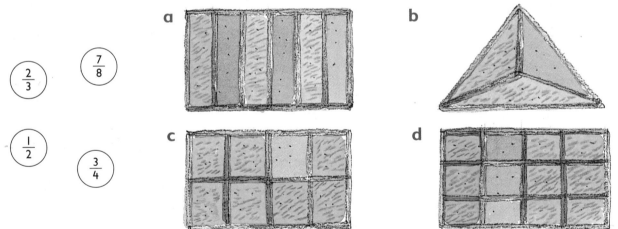

a b c d

4 Copy each field on to squared paper. Colour the fraction shown.

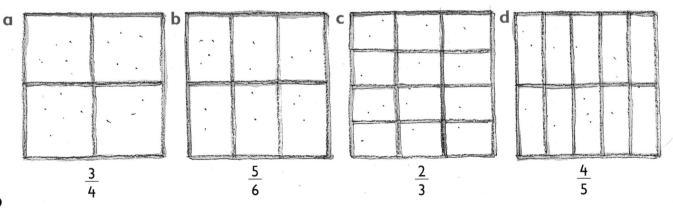

a $\frac{3}{4}$ b $\frac{5}{6}$ c $\frac{2}{3}$ d $\frac{4}{5}$

Lolly fractions

Refresher

1 Write down the number of lolly packs.

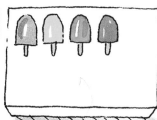

a

b

c

d

$3\frac{1}{4}$

Practice

1 Match each fraction to the lolly packs.

a

b

$1\frac{4}{5}$ $2\frac{3}{4}$

c

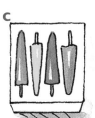  

$2\frac{3}{8}$ $1\frac{4}{10}$

d

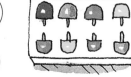 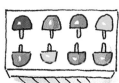 

2 This is a whole pack of ice cream.
   Draw these numbers of packs.

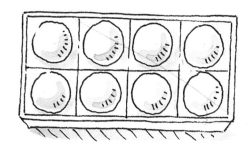

a $2\frac{1}{2}$ b $3\frac{1}{4}$ c $1\frac{3}{8}$ d $2\frac{3}{4}$ e $3\frac{7}{8}$

47

Freaky fraction machines

Refresher

1 Look at the instructions on the machines to calculate the
numbers coming out. Now write the calculations as fractions.

Example

a 10 ÷2 5 $\frac{1}{2}$

b 12 ÷3

c 16 ÷4

d 18 ÷2

e 24 ÷4

f 21 ÷3

g 36 ÷4

h 30 ÷3

i 16 ÷2

Practice

1 Write down the fraction of sweets that will go into each bag.
Now write the calculation as a division fact.

a

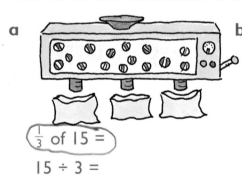

$\frac{1}{3}$ of 15 =

15 ÷ 3 =

b $\frac{1}{2}$ of 18

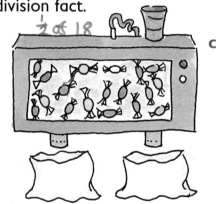

c $\frac{1}{4}$ of 32

2 Calculate the numbers coming out of the machines.

a 28 $\frac{1}{4}$

b 24 $\frac{1}{3}$

c 68 $\frac{1}{2}$

3 Calculate the amounts coming out of the machine.

a 76p $\frac{1}{2}$

b 24 cm $\frac{1}{4}$

c 90p $\frac{1}{2}$

d £1 $\frac{1}{4}$

e 1 m $\frac{1}{2}$

f 4 cm $\frac{1}{4}$

Cooking fractions

Refresher

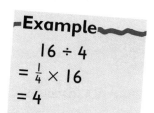

1 Work out these division facts. Now write each fact as a fraction calculation.

a $15 \div 5$

b $80 \div 10$

c $40 \div 5$

d $120 \div 10$

e $45 \div 5$

f $700 \div 10$

g $35 \div 5$

h $950 \div 10$

Practice

1 Find $\frac{1}{5}$ of each item of food. Now write your answer as a division fact.

a  30 g

b  25 ml

c  500 g

2 Find $\frac{1}{10}$ of each item of food. Now write your answer as a division fact.

a  70 g

b  300 ml

c  I kg

3 Match the fraction of £1 with a corresponding coin.

$\frac{1}{100}$ $\frac{1}{20}$ $\frac{1}{2}$

$\frac{1}{5}$ $\frac{1}{10}$

a

b

c

d

e

Artistic fractions

Refresher

1 Write Mary's crayons as a fraction of Liam's.

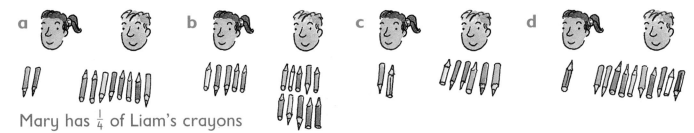

a   b   c   d

Mary has $\frac{1}{4}$ of Liam's crayons

Practice

2 What fraction of the large can is the small can?

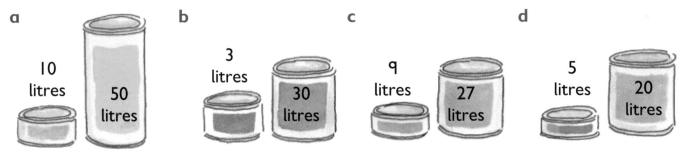

a   10 litres   50 litres

b   3 litres   30 litres

c   9 litres   27 litres

d   5 litres   20 litres

3 What fraction of £1 are these coins?

a   50   b   1   1   c   10   d   20   5

4. Write the missing fraction.

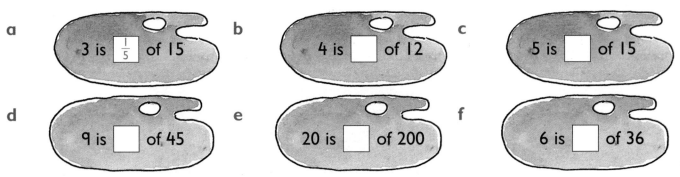

a   3 is $\frac{1}{5}$ of 15

b   4 is ☐ of 12

c   5 is ☐ of 15

d   9 is ☐ of 45

e   20 is ☐ of 200

f   6 is ☐ of 36

Find the difference

Refresher

1 Use the two 2-digit numbers to make one addition
   and one subtraction calculation.

a	24, 35	b	11, 37	c	46, 23
d	31, 48	e	32, 54	f	45, 35
f	55, 32	g	64, 23	h	75, 12
i	43, 48	j	69, 31	k	56, 13

Practice

1 Use the two 2-digit numbers to make one addition
   and one subtraction calculation.

a	57, 36	b	39, 47	c	62, 38
d	38, 63	e	68, 29	f	54, 47

2 Find the difference between these two
   numbers. Use an empty number line to
   help you if you need to.

Example

+3   +4

97   100   104   difference is 7

a 104, 97

b 156, 167

c 209, 191

d 287, 301

e 512, 498

f 674, 662

Addition facts

Lay out the calculations vertically then work out the answers. Add the units first.

Refresher

a 54 + 45 = ☐

b 68 + 17 = ☐

c 49 + 50 = ☐

d 55 + 34 = ☐

e 153 + 46 = ☐

f 237 + 52 = ☐

g 305 + 74 = ☐

h 412 + 73 = ☐

i 432 + 56 = ☐

j 526 + 61 = ☐

Practice

a 124 + 57 = ☐

b 234 + 48 = ☐

c 303 + 77 = ☐

d 418 + 75 = ☐

e 254 + 72 = ☐

f 368 + 81 = ☐

g 427 + 91 = ☐

h 531 + 86 = ☐

i 421 + 346 = ☐

j 537 + 256 = ☐

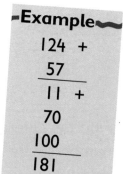

Take it away

Refresher

1 Write out each calculation vertically. Then partition
   the numbers and work out the answer.

a 85 – 42 = ☐

b 79 – 37 = ☐

c 184 – 62 = ☐

d 247 – 36 = ☐

e 296 – 71 = ☐

f 382 – 61 = ☐

g 478 – 57 = ☐

h 596 – 73 = ☐

i 587 – 62 = ☐

j 678 – 46 = ☐

k 688 – 54 = ☐

Practice

1 Write out each calculation vertically. Then partition the
   numbers and work out the answer. Adjust the tens or
   units if they cannot be subtracted.

a 276 – 59 = ☐

b 394 – 67 = ☐

c 486 – 48 = ☐

d 598 – 69 = ☐

e 485 – 193 = ☐

f 542 – 161 = ☐

g 625 – 183 = ☐

h 649 – 168 = ☐

i 753 – 475 = ☐

j 842 – 358 = ☐

Up to the minute

Refresher

Write the time on each clock in words.

1 a  b c d

2 a **8:14** b **6:25** c **1:09** d **12:16**

Practice

Example
3:43
Three forty three
Forty three minutes past three
Seventeen minutes to four

1 Write these times in three ways.

   a 2:58   b 4:56   c 6:49

   d 8:51   e 12:54   f 9:48

2 Copy and complete these time sequences.

   a   5:00   5:01   5:02   _____   _____   _____

   b   3:56   _____   3:58   _____   _____   _____   4:02

   c   12:25   12:27   _____   _____   _____   12:35

3 The time this clock shows is 9:16.
   What time will it show

   a in 2 hour's time

   b in half an hour

   c in 15 minutes

   d in 8 minutes

   e in 48 minutes?

4 Look at the time on this clock.

   Write in digital form the time

   a 3 hours earlier

   b 15 minutes earlier

   c half an hour later

54

● Use, read and write the vocabulary related to time
● Choose and use appropriate number operations and appropriate ways of calculating (mental, mental with jottings, paper and pencil) to solve problems

Au 11, 5

Measuring time

Refresher

1 Write which unit you would use to measure how long it takes to do these.

a boil an egg

b cross the road safely

c build a house

d blink

e run 100 metres

f eat an ice cream

2 Write the best estimate for these times.

a a bus journey into town	15 minutes	30 minutes	1 hour
b a fortnight's holiday	10 days	2 weeks	40 days
c a sneeze	2 seconds	20 seconds	40 seconds
d a flight to America from London	1 hour	3 hours	10 hours

Practice

Your group has 5 minutes at each station.

Make a chart in your exercise book to show what you did at each station.

Station	Activity	Estimated time	Measured time

Station 1	Station 2	Station 3
Estimate and measure the time taken: ● to read aloud a verse of a poem. ● for an ice cube to melt. ● for a dripping tap to fill a 100 ml jug.	Estimate and measure how many seconds it will take you to: ● say the 4 times table. ● build a tetrahedron with interlocking tiles. ● thread 10 wooden beads. ● touch your toes ten times.	● Choose a length of time between 10 and 30 seconds. Take it in turns to stop a stopwatch at that time without looking at the dial. ● Sit and face your partner. Stare into each other's eyes when the timekeeper says "Go". Who, in your group, can stare for the longest time?

Shopping tallies

Refresher

Mary asked people questions about shopping. She made a tally chart for each question. Copy the tally charts and write the frequencies. Now answer the questions for each chart.

1   a How many people shop at a mini-market?

    b What is the frequency for the supermarket?

    c What is the lowest frequency? What does this mean?

    d How many people did Mary ask altogether?

Which shop do you go to?

Shop	Tally	Frequency
mini-market	⅋⅋⅋ IIII	
supermarket	⅋⅋⅋ ⅋⅋⅋ III	
deli	⅋⅋⅋ II	
corner shop	⅋⅋⅋ ⅋⅋⅋ ⅋⅋⅋ III	

2   a Which is the most popular place to buy bread from?

    b How many people did Mary ask altogether?

    c How many more people bought bread from the baker than the milkman?

Where do you buy bread from?

Shop	Tally	Frequency
supermarket	⅋⅋⅋ ⅋⅋⅋ ⅋⅋⅋ I	
baker	⅋⅋⅋ ⅋⅋⅋ II	
milkman	⅋⅋⅋	
other shop	⅋⅋⅋ IIII	

3   Mary has rubbed out her tally marks.

    a Copy the tally chart.

    b Fill in the tally marks. Remember: use ⅋⅋⅋ for every 5 tally marks.

    c How many more people bought brown bread than wholemeal?

    d Which bread had the highest frequency? What does this mean?

What kind of bread do you buy?

Bread	Tally	Frequency
white		23
brown		13
wholemeal		9
granary		10

56

Practice

1 Play the Shopping game. You will need a counter and a 1–6 die.
- Put your counter on a shop.
- Throw the die and move clockwise.
- Make a tally mark for each shop you land on.
- Stop when one shop has 15 tally marks.

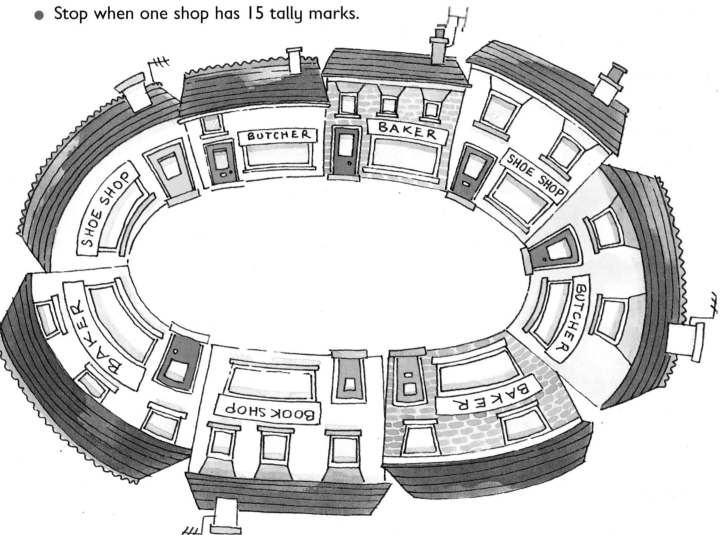

2 Complete your tally chart, then answer the questions.

a Which shop did you visit most?

b What is the lowest frequency? What does this mean?

c How many shops did you visit altogether?

Shops visited		
Shop	**Tally**	**Frequency**
baker		
butcher		
shoe shop		
book shop		

Musical pictograms

Refresher

1 Count the instruments then complete the tally chart.

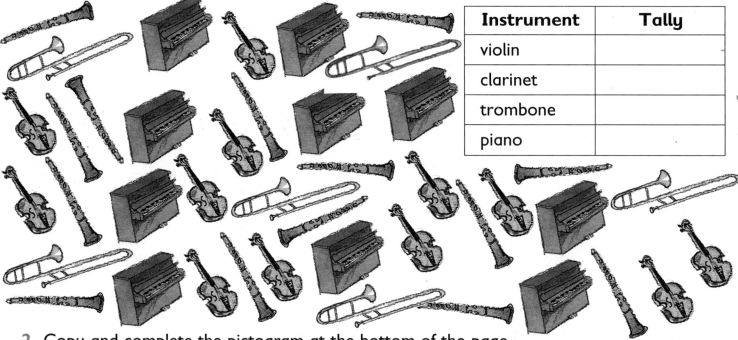

Instrument	Tally
violin	
clarinet	
trombone	
piano	

2 Copy and complete the pictogram at the bottom of the page.

3 Draw ♫ for every two instruments, then complete the key.

4 a How many violins are there?

   b Which is the least common instrument?

   c Which instrument has a frequency of 14?

   d What is the highest frequency? What does your answer mean?

Musical instruments							
violin							Key
clarinet							
trombone							
piano							

Practice

1 Count the tickets sold for each row then complete the frequency table.

Row	Frequency
A	
B	13
C	
D	

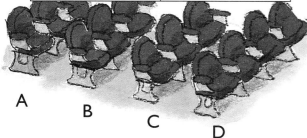

A   B   C   D

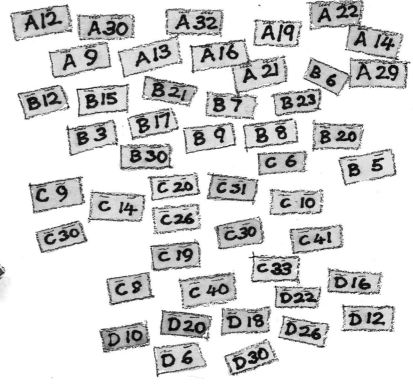

2 Copy and complete the pictogram at the bottom of the page.

3 Draw a simple picture for every two tickets, then complete the key.

4 a How many tickets were sold for row A?

  b Which row has most tickets sold?

  c Which row has a frequency of 11?

  d What is the lowest frequency? What does your answer mean?

Concert tickets sold

Row							Key
A							
B							
C							
D							

Word sorting

Refresher

The words are the names of fruit, animals, flowers and countries.

banana	hedgehog	hippopotamus	America	dog	dandelion	Africa
Germany	pig	grape	apple	lily	cow	Japan
bear	China	leopard	rabbit	Greece	England	monkey
cat	gorilla	rose	crocus	fox	rat	Russia
crocodile	lion	pear	Scotland	violet	France	mouse
sheep	India	tulip	ape	buttercup	snake	chimpanzee
Italy	tiger	sunflower	melon	Brazil	Spain	Australia
lizard	elephant	pansy	daffodil	pineapple	cheetah	hamster

1 a Copy the tally chart and make a tally mark for each word.

  b Count the tally marks. Now write the frequencies.

  c Copy and complete the pictogram. Use ✎ to represent five words.

Name	Tally	Frequency
Fruit		
Animal		
Flower		
Country		

Names								
Fruit								
Animal								
Flower								
Country								

Key: _____

2 a How many names of fruit are there?

  b What is the frequency of animal words?

  c What is the highest frequency? What does this tell you?

  d What is the lowest frequency? What does this tell you?

Practice

1 These words begin with vowels.

apple   **e**xtra   **i**f   **o**ver   **u**pon

a Copy the tally chart.

b Use a reading book to find words that begin with vowels. Make a tally mark for each vowel. Stop when one letter has a frequency of between 30 and 35.

Vowel	Tally	Frequency
a		
e		
i		
o		
u		

c Count the tally marks then write the frequencies.

d Copy and complete the pictogram. Choose your own picture to represent five words.

Vowels words begin with							
a							
e							
i							
o							
u							

Key: _____

2 **a** How many words begin with **e**?

   b What is the frequency for **a**?

   c What is the highest frequency? What does this tell you?

   d Which vowel occurs the least?

Counter counting

Refresher

1 a Cover this page with different-coloured counters.
      For each colour, make piles of ten counters.

   b Copy and complete this
      frequency table.

   c Copy and complete the
      pictogram. Use ◯ to represent
      ten counters.

Colour	Frequency
Red	

Coloured counters

Red							

Key: _____ represents _____

2 a How many red counters are there?

   b What is the frequency for yellow counters?

   c What is the highest frequency? What does this tell you?

   d What is the lowest frequency? What does this tell you?

Practice

1 Count the coins and notes.

35

30

15

55

a Copy and complete the frequency table.

b Copy and complete the pictogram. Choose your own picture to represent 10 coins or notes.

Coin/Note	Frequency
£1	

Coins and notes

£1								

Key: _____ represents _____

2 a How many £1 coins are there?

b What is the frequency for £10 notes?

c What is the highest frequency? What does this tell you?

d How many notes are there altogether?

e What is the least frequent note?

Fairground pictograms

Refresher

The children in class 4A voted for their favourite ride.

1 Copy and complete the pictogram. Use 😊 to represent 2 rides.

Ride	Frequency
Rollercoaster	14
House of horrors	5
Bumper cars	13
Swingboat	11

Favourite fairground ride

Rollercoaster								
House of horrors								
Bumper cars								
Swingboat								

Key: _____

2 a How many children voted for the swingboat?

  b What is the frequency for the rollercoaster?

Practice

The table shows you how many times the children went on a ride.

1 Copy and complete the pictogram. Use 😊 to represent 5 rides.

Ride	Frequency
Rollercoaster	40
House of horrors	15
Bumper cars	23
Swingboat	10

Favourite fairground ride

Rollercoaster								
House of horrors								
Bumper cars								
Swingboat								

Key: _____ represents _____

2. a How many children went on the rollercoaster?

  b What is the frequency for the bumper cars?